W9-ATP-496

First Facts®

Investigating
CONTINENTS
EUROPE
A 4D Book

by Christine Juarez

PEBBLE
a capstone imprint

Download the Capstone 4D app!

- Ask an adult to download the Capstone 4D app.
- Scan the cover and stars inside the book for additional content.

When you scan a spread, you'll find
fun extra stuff to go with this book!
You can also find these things
on the web at www.capstone4D.com
using the password: europe.27988

First Facts are published by Pebble,
1710 Roe Crest Drive, North Mankato, Minnesota 56003
www.mycapstone.com

Library of Congress Cataloging-in-Publication Data
Names: Juarez, Christine, 1976– author.
Title: Europe : a 4D book / by Christine Juarez.
Description: North Mankato, Minnesota : Pebble, 2019. | Series: First facts. Investigating continents
Identifiers: LCCN 2018004057 (print) | LCCN 2018011046 (ebook) | ISBN 9781543528107 (eBook PDF) |
ISBN 9781543527988 (hardcover) | ISBN 9781543528046 (pbk.)
Subjects: LCSH: Europe—Geography—Juvenile literature.
Classification: LCC D900 (ebook) | LCC D900 .J83 2019 (print) | DDC 914—dc23
LC record available at https://lccn.loc.gov/2018004057

Editorial Credits
Cynthia Della-Rovere and Clare Webber, designers; Svetlana Zhurkin, media researcher;
Kathy McColley, production specialist

Photo Credits
Capstone Global Library Ltd, 5, 9; Newscom: picture-alliance/dpa/Andreas Gebert, 21; Shutterstock:
Aleksandr Pobedimskiy, 13, Alexey Poprotskiy, 9 (inset), Calin Stan, 15, GarryKillian (pattern), cover (left)
and throughout, Gen_Shtab, 11, kavram, 17, Lasse Mehrfeld, 7, Lightspring, cover (bottom right), back cover,
1, 3, Ondrej Prosicky, cover (bottom left), Stanislav Duben, 14, Stefan Sorean, cover (top), Yuri Turkov, 19,
Zoltan Gabor, cover (middle)

Printed and bound in the USA.   PA017

Table of Contents

About Europe

Europe is a small **continent**. Only the continent of Australia is smaller than Europe.

Europe has a big neighbor to the east. It's Asia, the largest continent. On the west side of Europe is the Atlantic Ocean. The Mediterranean Sea lies to the south and the Arctic Ocean is to the north. Many islands in these oceans are also a part of Europe.

PACIFIC OCEAN

continent—one of Earth's seven large land masses

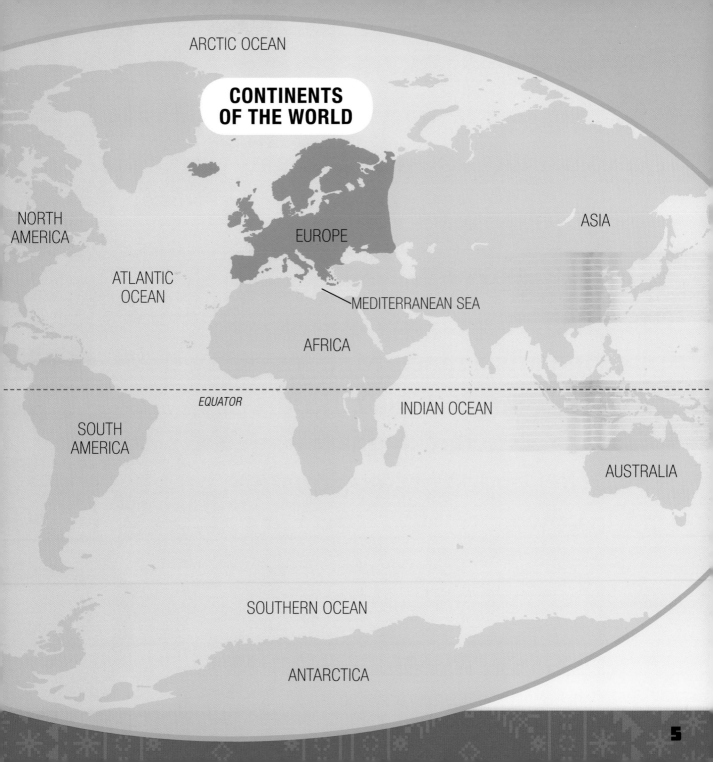

ARCTIC OCEAN

CONTINENTS OF THE WORLD

NORTH AMERICA

ASIA

EUROPE

ATLANTIC OCEAN

MEDITERRANEAN SEA

AFRICA

EQUATOR

INDIAN OCEAN

SOUTH AMERICA

AUSTRALIA

SOUTHERN OCEAN

ANTARCTICA

Famous Places

There are many well-known places in Europe. The Colosseum in Rome, Italy, is a huge arena where **gladiators** fought. It was built almost 2,000 years ago. The Eiffel Tower is a famous place in Paris, France. Millions of tourists visit it each year. People may also go to Buckingham Palace in London or Red Square in Moscow.

The Colosseum

gladiator—a man in Ancient Rome who fought against another man or animal in order to entertain a crowd

Geography

Mountains are found in Europe. The Alps stretch from France to Austria. Europe's highest mountain is Mount Elbrus in the Caucasus Mountains.

There are some active volcanoes in Europe. Mount Etna is on the island of Sicily, in Italy. It **erupts** every few years. There are more than 30 active volcanoes in the small country of Iceland.

Fact: Europe is the only continent with no deserts.

erupt—to burst out suddenly with great force

ICELAND

LANDFORMS OF EUROPE

N
W · E
S

Mount Elbrus

Alps

Caucasus Mountains

Mount Etna

Rivers are important in Europe. Ships travel between cities on these rivers. The Volga is the continent's longest river. The Rhine and the Danube flow through the middle of Europe.

Europe has many large lakes. Lake Ladoga in Russia is the largest lake. It is 136 miles (219 kilometers) across. There are also stunning lakes in the mountains of Switzerland and Italy.

Fact: The Volga River is 2,300 miles (3,701 km) long.

Volga River

Weather

Europe has all kinds of weather. In the far north, it is always cold and icy. Around the Mediterranean Sea, Europe's weather is hot and sunny in summer. In most of Europe, summers are warm and winters are cool. It can be rainy at any time of year.

The country of Greece has many warm, sunny beaches along the Mediterranean Sea.

Animals

Different animals live in different parts of Europe. Wolves, bears, deer, and foxes are animals that live in northern Europe. Polar bears, seals, and reindeer are in the cold Arctic parts of Europe.

There are also birds, like the golden eagle in Europe's mountains. In the **delta** of the Danube River live flamingos, pelicans, and many other types of birds.

red fox

delta—an area of land shaped like a triangle where a river meets a sea or an ocean

pelicans

Plants

Thick green forests grow in northern Europe. Pine and fir trees grow there. Farther south are forests of oaks and beeches.

Different types of plants grow in the far south. The weather is warmer and drier there. Olives, lemons, and oranges grow on trees. People grow grapes on vines in vineyards.

Tall pine trees grow in Finland, a country in far northern Europe.

People

There are 45 countries in Europe. About 743 million people live there. Russia is the largest country, even though only part of it is in Europe. The rest is in Asia. Vatican City in Rome is the smallest country in the world. Most countries in Europe have their own language.

London, Moscow, and Paris are three of the biggest cities in Europe. They are the capital cities of the United Kingdom, Russia, and France.

London, England,
United Kingdom

Natural Resources and Products

Many **natural resources** and **industries** are in Europe. Trees are grown for their wood. Coal is a fuel used to make electricity. It is dug from the ground in Russia, Germany, and Poland. Fashion is a big industry in Europe and shows take place in major cities. Car companies like Volkswagen, BMW, and Audi started in Germany. The products made in Europe are sold around the world.

natural resource—a material from nature that is useful to people

industry—a set of businesses that make a living in the same way

A worker puts together a car at a factory in Germany.

Glossary

continent (KAHN-tuh-nuhnt)—one of Earth's seven large land masses

delta (DEL-tuh)—an area of land shaped like a triangle where a river enters a sea or ocean

erupt (i-RUHPT)—to burst out suddenly with great force

gladiator (GLAD-ee-ay-tur)—a person from Ancient Rome who fought against other gladiators or animals in order to entertain a crowd

industry (IN-duh-stree)—a set of businesses that make a living the same way

natural resource (NACH-ur-uhl REE-sorss)—a material from nature that is useful to people

Read More

Oachs, Emily Rose. *Europe.* Discover the Continents. Minneapolis: Bellwether Media, Inc.: 2016.

Sherman, Jill. *Continents: What You Need to Know.* Fact Files. North Mankato, Minn.: Capstone Press, 2017.

Internet Sites

Use FactHound to find Internet sites related to this book.

Visit *www.facthound.com*

Just type in 9781543527988 and go.

Check out projects, games and lots more at
www.capstonekids.com

Critical Thinking Questions

1. London, Moscow, and Paris are three of the biggest cities in Europe. In which countries can you find these cities?

2. Why are rivers important in Europe?

3. What kinds of landforms are in Europe? Where can they be found?

Index